Strange Metal
Bouquet

Pamela Adams

For Leona & Nazaire

This book is dedicated to:
every fork in the road that led me here
and anyone who has ever loved and lost
and found what sustains them

May these carefully-placed words
be a trail of breadcrumbs leading you home.

Contents

STRANGE METAL BOUQUET

Stream of Consciousness #1

We're supposed to write like we're chasing a train...nonstop thoughts...don't look back at what you left behind. If we keep running, the past can't catch up. Running towards something or away from. We carry our heavy baggage assuming we'll unpack when we get there. Things always get lost along the way. Whether the clasp is broken and the feelings spill out or the weight of it all threatens to pull our shoulder clean out of its socket. We keep throwing punches that never quite land where we aim. Our arms grow weary...too weary to reach out...too weak to pull the fire alarm. There is something burning, but we'd have to run all the way into the center to find it. As the doors slam closed behind us...the friends and lovers turned strangers wave as we pass. A solo parade...a last ride on a thirsty horse called Truth...lies tossed like confetti litter the streets...running too fast to stop and sweep the mess under the carpet, baggage bouncing awkwardly against my leg... that's gonna leave a mark. Hands calloused from gripping the handle so tightly. Showing you my palms...nothing up my sleeve...sleight of hand...revealing belly from supine position...the pen needs to keep running across the page. There's ink in the water...like a frightened octopus escaping from the enemy...the ink confuses...yet ink gets tattooed in the skin because everyone has a story to tell and some people wear their broken hearts on their sleeve... some people watch the ink flow like blood because broken hearts speak even without a mouth. Scars tell stories. Our belly button is our first scar...mouths screaming, "I'M ALIVE!"...telling our story of the day we were born...the first of many days we survived the blood and the truth and the solo parade out of our mother into waiting hands... darkness into light. We'd have a lifetime to accumulate our baggage and learn to bend with our knees so we don't get hurt carrying the load. We shapeshift under the burden from baby to adolescent and back to that hospital bed... and all the stops in between and the hands waiting to hold ours...a gentle anchor to tether us here because we are never alone. On the day we are born, our mother is always there and if you believe in God, our Father is there when we die. Life is perfect balance...the inhale and exhale...inspiration and expiration...we are either here or we're nowhere...now here.

Full Moon Interrogation

I think the best conversations
happen under a starry night sky.
With the full moon shining down on me
like an interrogation lamp,
I have no choice
but to tell you the truth.

My Father Forgets

My father forgets...
to put his coat on before walking outside
on a rainy morning.
He forgets what day of the week it is.
Once, he even forgot my birthday.
I always have to remind him how to
work the DVD player,
and I patiently listen to the same stories
every time I see him,
knowing that one day,
I will long
to hear them all again.

My father forgets...
so sometimes he doesn't realize that his left hand
is still curled tightly
around his shredded dinner napkin...
the way it once curled around mine
as I walked beside him,
trying to keep up...
and so I wonder if he remembers the day
his car broke down near the railroad tracks
and, realizing that I was barefoot,
he carried me on his back the entire way home.

My father forgets...
but I remember.

A Thousand Times a Day

I fall in love
a thousand times a day—
while watching an old man in a red cardigan
cross the street
relying heavily on his cane,
or seeing a hawk
soar high above a cemetery,
or a mangy dog
roaming my neighborhood
without a leash.
These things often break my heart
just as easily.

My Stories

My stories
start out dangerous
with jagged edges,
yet through
the constant retelling,
they have been
worn smooth
like sea glass
and are actually
quite beautiful
when the light shines through.

HELP!

Like the little boy who cried "WOLF!",
the old man across the hall
often yells, "HELP!"
and the nurses seldom come running.
Maybe they don't believe him anymore,
yet I still peek in on him
just to be sure.
I think that one word
has become a mantra to him,
a way to comfort himself
when he's feeling
lonely or afraid.
What I've learned
while visiting the nursing home
these past few years is
that when the sun goes down,
or when their inner light
starts to dim,
they all cry out
for their mother.

Rain Haiku

When the rain comes down,
I find that I am not so
impermeable.

I'd like to believe
that I have fixed all the holes
where the rain gets in.

Sometimes there's a flood.
It's so easy to give up
with all this water.

Yet at other times,
just enough rain is released
to nurture what's there.

"All you need is love"...
love and possibly just a
better umbrella.

Daisies

As babies,
we all have that
innate grasping reflex.
From the moment we are born,
we instinctively know how
to reach out for what we need
to sustain us
and hold on tightly.
It's a shame that at some point
we lose this.
Holding on is easy.
We have to *learn* how to let go.
I like the imagery
of a fistful of daisies...
"he loves me...he loves me not".
So often our hands are clenched in anger
or because we are not yet ready
to let go of something...
or some*one*...
but a fistful of daisies
is like transforming anger
into forgiveness.
That's beautiful.
That's ~ALCHEMY~.
I just want someone
to stand on the doorstep of my heart
and offer me something
simple and beautiful.

Tongue Tied

I get tongue tied.
I toss my words like confetti.
I want him to celebrate me,
but he only sees the mess
he'd have to clean up later.

Love Letter

The love letter begins
long before
the pen touches the page,
like fingertips tracing
bare skin...
love is slowly being written
with indelible ink...
flowing...in the gentle pull
of my ocean's pulse...
in the way the persistent waves
shape the rocks...
smoothing all the jagged edges
of yesterday's heartache.
All I have is
what I bring
to this moment
Breath becomes words.
Soul mingling with the soil
of deep consciousness.
When I see with my heart,
everything I do
becomes a love letter.

(Hug)

When he reached out
to hug me,
his arms were shaped
like parentheses.
Maybe that's why
the rest of the world
fell silent
while I was tucked into
his embrace.

Random Thoughts About Running

Random thoughts about running...
Love is a marathon,
and I've always been
more of a sprinter.
I've been running for so long
I've gotten used to the feeling of
being out of breath.
There are some days
when I no longer believe that
there will ever be someone
waiting for me
at the end of the day,
arms wide open
like a finish line.

Strange Metal Bouquet

I like things
that play tug of war with my emotions...
times when I have the opportunity to smile
while my heart is breaking...
like when the woman with dementia
painstakingly removes
an impressive collection of silverware
from her purse
and lines it all up on the table.
and then,
just as I start to feel a little sad,
she gathers all the utensils in her fist,
smiles
and offers them to the old man
sitting across from her, like some
strange metal bouquet.

Stones

One day,
I was walking along the beach...
no, not with the Lord,
with some guy Mike....
and we would occasionally bend
to pick up tiny, shiny pebbles,
like Hansel & Gretel in reverse—
and I started thinking
about different stones in history,
like the ones Virginia Woolf
filled her pockets with
before walking into the river,
or the one David
tucked into his slingshot
before he slew the giant Goliath,
or the sparkly ones
offered on bended knee.

Slow Shuffle

My father has dementia.
I think of the man he once was...
the way his glasses slid
halfway down his nose
as he sat at the kitchen table
reading the newspaper every morning...
the man who used to
spontaneously recite Rudyard Kipling's "If"...
the one who inspired me
to become a better writer.
I look at him now...
this shy, intelligent man
who has known me my entire life,
and I wonder
how much time we have left together...
before he doesn't remember me at all,
before he forgets everything,
before I lose him completely.
I watch him
slowly shuffle
across the room...
his frail body
curved like a question mark
as he clings to his walker.
Sometimes
there are no answers.

Names Are Magic

Names are magic.
In fairy tales,
naming is knowledge.
("RUMPLESTILTSKIN!")
I once walked
through a cemetery,
reading the names
on the tombstones and
reciting them aloud.
It began to sound
like some
magical incantation.
People whose names
had not been spoken for
over a hundred years...
people who
no longer had anyone
alive left to mourn them...
in that brief moment,
they were
resurrected
when I
spoke their
names.

Roam

In my dreams of aching wanderlust,
I walk abandoned cities of Rome...
seeking what eludes me,
searching for my home.
I travel smooth, forgotten streets
well-worn from tourists and time,
surrounded by sweet memories.
I drink them in like wine.
I pause in a dark cathedral
to rest my weary bones.
Within I find divinity,
and I will call it home.

Love Always Wins

Ever since my dad
had his second stroke,
the limp in his gait has
become more pronounced.
He drags his left leg
when he walks.
So earlier today,
while helping him
get to the bathroom...
I held him,
he held his walker...
I slid my right toe
under his left heel,
lifting it for him.
We participated in
the world's slowest
three-legged race.
Love always wins.

Elderly Woman Dancing

Today,
I watched an elderly woman in a wheelchair
prove that you *can* still dance
while in a seated position.
She was listening to Irish music.
Her eyes were closed,
her hands, slowly swaying side to side
as though she was conducting an invisible orchestra...
and she was SMILING.
As I watched her feet
barely lifting off the ground
in time to the rhythm,
for a moment,
it was like staring
directly into the sun.
I had to look away.
My eyes were beginning to water.

My Daddy Used to Sing...

My daddy used to sing
to me...
push me high on the swing...
to me,
he was everything...
chauffeur, mechanic,
dealer of cards,
watcher of Wiffle ball games
in our backyard,
eater of Hoodsie cups,
feeder of birds,
newspaper reader,
lover of words,
reciter of Kipling,
funny and wise,
hard worker,
soft hearted...
the bluest of eyes...
kite maker, dreamer,
always longing to fly...
warm hearted,
yet cold,
so he kept the thermostat high.
egg burner...bless his heart...
that man could *not* cook,
but he was friends with the squirrels,
so he's okay in my book.

In photos,
we dance, arm wrestle, and play.
I've captured his smile
to remind me someday
what it looked like
those times
when we spoke face to face...
and what it felt like
to sit there
and be loved
in that space.

Red Pen Poem

I wish all our red pens would run out of ink.
You see your "thunder thighs".
I see the old friend who showed up today,
walking towards me.
You cover your mouth to hide your teeth,
but I only hear the laughter
that escapes around your fingers,
which have texted me on days
when I least expected it
and most needed it.
You think you're fat.
I say you give the best hugs.
You pinch your midsection and frown,
and I marvel that your body
made *two* babies.

I want to fire our inner critics.
That job became obsolete.
Who hired them in the first place?
You think you are just the accumulation of
every negative comment
anyone has ever given you.
You are every copper penny tossed into a fountain.
I wish you would throw your red pen away.

Faces

I like to think of faces
as the covers to our books.
My friends' faces contain
some of my favorite stories.

When you hold me,
it feels like we are
two pages in the same story
and my heart is a rose petal
being gently pressed in between them.

Real Eyes

Did you not
realize
when something good
came along?...
because all the signs read
"High Voltage"
and the exits were gone
and too many people
had already left.
So you sat and drank coffee
and tried to make art
while you waited for
love to show up,
not realizing
that you are already both.

108 Doors

Some people believe
there are 108 doors
to our heart.
I like to imagine
there are just as many keys / ways to open them.
The keys may be shaped
like guitar picks,
or paint brushes.
I might even try to pick the lock
with a pair of knitting needles,
yet there are days when I inevitably
arrive at the last,
innermost door
and find that I'm all out of keys.
I have nothing left to offer,
and I feel like a stranger,
begging on the doorstep
of my own heart.
It is at this moment
when I remind myself
that even though my hands are empty,
I can still knock
and let myself in.

Thumb / Index

The thumb
and index finger,
when combined,
can be used for
all sorts of things...
dunking an Oreo in milk,
plucking white cat hair
off of black corduroys,
and strumming
a ukulele.

Wonder

Sometimes
when I just stand there
softly gazing up
at the night sky,
I remember
being small
and feeling the same
sense of wonder
while watching
my father shave.

Savasana

He was all
breath and light...
fading slowly...
while my mother,
now ashes and bone,
and I
played a
gentle game of
tug of war.
We have both come here
to claim him.
We stop
fighting the clock...
hands up...
surrender.
We wait.
There is nothing
left to do
but rest.

Midnight

Midnight is my favorite time.
Sometimes spells are broken and the magic wears off.
Sometimes there's someone to kiss when the ball drops,
but one day always becomes the next at midnight,
and we each have a chance to begin all over again.

Dentures

My mom told me
my dad lost
his bottom dentures.
We surmised he went to bed
without removing them
and speculated about
where they could be.
I suggested
maybe the laundry room
will find them
rolled up in his sheets.
She asked,
"How will they know
who they belong to?"
I told her,
"Maybe it'll be
like Cinderella,
and they'll just
walk around,
trying them on,
and when they get to Dad,
they'll magically fit.

The Day Before

On the day
before my mother died,
I sat beside her,
knitting
while we listened to
Elvis sing gospel
through my phone
resting beside her
on her pillow.
The words that were
too sad to say
became stitches...
clicking needles,
a Morse code
to my mother's heart.
"I love you."
"I'll miss you."
"Thank you."
Save your words.
Mouths don't matter
and time doesn't exist here—
only love.

Grief is Heavy

Grief is heavy.
It weighs me down...
makes me feel like I'm
walking around wearing one of those
lead aprons,
but x-rays are for taking a closer look inside,
examining
what needs to be healed.

Steven

When I was in elementary school,
there was a little boy
on my bus
named Steven.
Some of the bigger kids
used to make fun of him
because he had
one of those strawberry birthmarks
that covered
almost half his face,
like a dark pink
Phantom of the Opera mask.
I noticed the way
his brown eyes
were always
too shy
to meet
anyone else's.
I asked my mom
what happened to him.
She told me,
"his mother had a
very hard time
bringing him
into this world.
She almost died."

There but for the
grace of God go I
because had she listened
to all those people
trying to discourage her from
having a baby at 44,
I probably
wouldn't be here.
So every time
those kids
laughed at him,
I know
they only saw
the birthmark,
but I saw
the miracle
because my mother
taught me
where to look.
Do you believe in miracles?
Have you forgotten
that you *are* one?

Stream of Consciousness #2

You can be flexible like the sway of the trees. Your breath could exhale like that steady breeze. It could float through your hair or ripple the dog-eared pages of your notebooks. Hold pen like sword...or a surgeon's scalpel... incising/excising...removing the tumor of your fear... and all the memories that have calcified and blocked the exit, prevent the admittance of any search team. Admit that we are missing...or that we are wanted...hang posters everywhere...someone is always searching for us...is this why people take so many selfies now? They don't want to be forgotten? Outlaws are immortal. Don't be afraid to show your face. Be front-page news...even if you're the only person who reads the articles. Write a ransom note if you have to...to recover yourself...demand your return... you know this disappearance is only temporary...you keep looking...and you catch your reflection in the mirror...the wanted poster hanging on your own wall.

Captured

I woke up on New Year's Day 2018
with a profound sense of sadness.
The emptiness of
losing my mom
reminded me of
when I play chess and
someone captures my queen.
I don't even want to play
anymore.
The most important piece
of the whole game,
and now the king
is unprotected.

Looking for Leona

In his wheelchair,
he uses his good hand
to pull himself along
the confusing corridors
of his mind.
Everyone who walks by
has possible information.
He asks them all
if they've seen her.
He is crestfallen.
"Five minutes feels like two hours."
She has been missing
all day.
She's not in the dining room.
He's surprised
she hasn't joined us for lunch.
Maybe she's playing bingo.
We can't find her there,
yet we keep searching...
because he is worried...
and he wants to find her...
the slowest,
saddest
game of Hide 'N' Seek.

Hummingbirds

The largest hummingbird
weighs 21 grams.
I once read that this
is the same amount of weight
we lose when we die.
Now I'm sure there's some
scientific explanation for that
(breath escaping our lungs,
bladder emptying),
but I like to imagine
it's our soul leaving our body.
So when I marvel that a tiny hummingbird
weighs the same as our soul,
it really impresses upon me
how fragile they are...
how fragile we *all* are.

ENCORE

A Bouquet of Roses

Sun & Moon

During the lowest points of this past year, when it felt like I was drowning, I searched for anything that was a constant. I started small. I looked up at the stars. I often stopped to admire the sky. I knew for a fact that the sun would rise every morning and every night the moon would be right where I left it. This I could rely on, and it brought me the first bit of comfort.

When my parents died,...my mother, the sun...giver of life and brightest source of love...and my father, the gentle moon...ensconced in shadows, basking in her glow, reflecting her light...the only two, true constants I've ever known fell from my sky and everything was absolute darkness...except I seemed to be the only one who noticed. Through the numb fog of grief, I watched life while moving in slow motion. The mail was delivered, the cat was hungry, and Alex Trebek kept requesting answers in the form of a question, yet still I was silent. I couldn't understand how the world could keep spinning when mine had completely lost its axis. I now realize that the world itself was a constant. It had to stay exactly the way it was so when I was ready to come back to it, it would be exactly the way I left it. Except now, my eyes have adjusted to all that darkness. Now I see the subtle colors shifting on the horizon and even the smallest act of kindness does not escape my attention.

My parents loved me.

This is my one, true constant.

Mother is the Name for God...

"Mother is the name for God on the lips and hearts of all children."

—William Makepeace Thackeray

When you lose your mother, the doorway through which you entered the world disappears. So one day, I was sitting in that dark, empty room with no exit...let's call it Grief... and I was thinking about how both my mom and dad were now gone. A tiny spark ignited. In what I can only file under "epiphany", some dormant truth slowly floated to the surface. It was the same feeling we seek when we enter a church...let's call it Divinity...the my soul tipping its imaginary hat to your soul. I realized that I hadn't really lost either of them because we were made of the same ingredients...whatever it is, they will always be a part of me...and I remembered how God was so clever that He hid a piece of Himself inside each of us because He knew that was the last place we would look. I found my mom... right where she'd always been hiding.

90

2/23/20

My mother would have celebrated her 90th birthday today. (That's *quatre-vingt dix* if you speak French...or four twenties and a ten if you're good at math.) I showed up almost exactly halfway through her life, but they say it's the quality of time we have here, not the quantity.

Sometimes random memories will sneak up on me... mostly good...and I'll stop to think of her.

My mother loved to sing...often LOUDLY!...especially in church. (I think maybe she just wanted to make sure God could hear her.) This was kind of embarrassing for a small, quiet kid who recoiled from the spotlight. However, she was also the same mom who, when I was 13 and waited hours for a friend who never showed up, took me to see *Over the Top* instead...just the two of us. (Well, three if you count Stallone...and I always do.) She was a good friend like that.

Memory

Sometimes I think about how John Keats said, "touch has a memory." I know this is true because every time I visited my dad, I would greet him with a kiss high on his cheekbone...three quick pecks, actually, because one didn't seem like enough...or maybe it was a subliminal "I. love. you." Anyway, I must've done this thousands of times, and one day, I showed up and he was taking a nap. I kissed his cheek. XXX Without even opening his eyes, he sleepily murmured, "Pa...me...la." It is often these brief moments where we are fully present that end up becoming the most transcendent ways we show someone they are loved.

Mother's Day 2020

My mother loved babies. She always knew what to do to relieve their belly aches and how to hold them to make them fall asleep instantly...her open arms like gates to some peaceful place.

I'd gape in wild wonder as she fearlessly jammed her knuckle into a teething infant's screaming mouth... sacrificing an index finger to appease the dental gods...as it gnawed and drooled in satisfaction all over her hand, spilling onto her pants.

When sticky-fingered grandchildren ran towards my mom, reaching out to her, I'd watch in abject horror as she picked them up and reassured everyone, "it's okay... I'm washable." (I still think of this every time someone apologizes as their dog slobbers all over me. Now, I often add, "Dog can't hold its licker.")

Several years ago, I asked my mom what she wanted for Mother's Day. Her answer was always the same...every birthday, every Christmas. It was always, "You. I just want all my kids to visit me."

At the time, I had been working on a bunch of miniature quilts for tiny babies who were stillborn or premature. I told her I would bring them to the hospital where she had me and donate them in her honor. I've continued to do this every year since that conversation. (I secretly like to think of those babies as "Leona's angels" because I know that she is somewhere taking care of all of them...or at least greeting them at the gates.)

This past February 23rd, on what would have been her 90th birthday, my sister came to the hospital with me to donate the blankets. As I offered them to the nurse, I told her why we were there:

"My mother was Leona. Today would have been her 90th birthday. I was born here."

Maybe I just wanted to go back to the place where we met... the first place I saw her...instead of the last. By speaking my mother's name aloud to a stranger and remembering the day she was born, this is how I keep her alive.

Tail Lights

I remember when I first started driving, and then after I moved out and went back to visit...I'd pull into the driveway, and, before I'd even turned my car off, my dad would be outside, ready to pop the hood, check the oil, top off the washer fluid, etc. I used to think to myself, "He's my one-man pit crew!" I miss those days.

And I always thought it was so sweet that he'd stand in the window and wave "goodbye" whenever I left. So one time, I asked him, "Why do you always watch me leave?" He said, "I wanna see if your tail lights are out."

Pierced

Sometimes my mother would raise an empty fork to her lips. I don't know if she realized there was no food on it, but I would admire the way, despite being blind, she kept trying, keeping faith in things she could not see. Most of the time, I wouldn't intervene. I would just silently bear witness, the way you patiently wait for a toddler to do just about anything, as you internally cheer from the sidelines. There is a learning process taking place. With my mom, she was the one teaching me.

Often, I would watch her take a bite as, once again, she completely missed the mark. Each persistent tine pierced my heart. Sometimes, I would use my own fork to push all the remaining food closer together on her plate, increasing her chances for success.

I watched her gnarled fingers, coiled around silver, as she lowered her hand to slowly stab in the vicinity of a potato. I remember those same hands pushing a rolling pin back and forth across thick dough as I peered over the top of our kitchen table. My tiny fingers reached out to swirl patterns in the dusty flour.

After she pressed the fork down all around the circumference of the pie to seal all the edges, she would coat the top of the crust by dipping the middle and ring fingers of her right hand into a shallow bowl of milk, the same graceful gesture she used to dab the Holy water from every font upon entering every church I'd ever followed her into, the same anointing of all that needed to be blessed. Mother, milk and sacrament. She taught me there is something Holy about feeding someone you love.

About the Author

Pamela Adams is a fabric artist born in Albion, Rhode Island. In addition to being fascinated by animals and hoping Hollywood never remakes *The Princess Bride*, she spends most of her free time increasing the mileage on her sewing machine's odometer.

Quilting is the perfect metaphor for anyone who has ever felt fragmented within themselves and tried to reintegrate back into society. After experiencing the loss of both elderly parents at the beginning of 2018, she collected all the salvaged pieces of her tattered heart, lovingly reassembled them and transformed her grief by slowly moving forward one stitch, and one word, at a time.

Strange Metal Bouquet is her first published collection.